Prayer-Bytes

Everyday Prayers for Young People

Rosemary and Peter Atkins

with illustrations by

Olivia Jackson-Mee

VERITAS

Prayer-Bytes was first published in 2004 by St Aidan's Parish, Remuera, Auckland, New Zealand in an edition entitled *Cool Prayers* for distribution in New Zealand and Australia. It is already in its second printing. International rights are licensed to other publishers for their regions of the world. This edition is published by Veritas Publications Ltd of Dublin for the regions of the United Kingdom, Northern Ireland and the Republic of Ireland.

ISBN 1 85390 917 3
Published 2006 by
Veritas Publications
7/8 Lower Abbey Street
Dublin 1
Ireland
Email publications@veritas.ie
Website www.veritas.ie

A catalogue record for this book is available from the British Library.

Printed in the Republic of Ireland by Betaprint, Dublin

Veritas books are printed on paper made from the wood pulp of managed forests. For every tree felled, at least one tree is planted, thereby renewing natural resources.

Prayers for Everyday

Contents

Thanks

The authors wish to express their thanks to:

Olivia Jackson-Mee for again joining them in a project to help young people pray and creating such wonderful interpretive illustrations for these prayers for her own age group;

Their parish of St Aidan for their continuing support in publishing these books of prayers;

Lloyd Brooks and Olivia Jackson-Mee who acted as junior advisors for the text, offering comments and suggestions as the prayers were composed. The text prayer (p. 9) was drafted by Lloyd;

A group of young people from the parish who put forward topics for inclusion in the section 'In Conversation with God' and expressed the need for verses from Scripture;

Hundreds of parishes, children and families who bought and use *Family Prayers*, and thus encouraged the production of this sequel volume.

And for this new edition, the Editor and her staff at Veritas Publications for their enthusiasm and skill in helping this book reach young people in their region.

So we pray that Prayer-Bytes will inspire young people in their developing relationship with God in prayer. To God be the thanks and the glory.
Peter and Rosemary Atkins.

Prayers *for* Everyday

Note on 'Daily Prayer'

Followers of Jesus Christ pray each day to remember God's presence and power in their lives. Prayer on waking and prayer before sleep are ways of framing the day as belonging to God and of showing that we know how close God is to us. During the day we offer prayers at significant moments – in a crisis situation, when we make mistakes, when we need strength to seize opportunities and when we want to thank God for all the good we receive. Today, in the time of text messages, our prayers can be short and to the point. In that way throughout the day we keep God up to date with all that is happening in our lives.

These daily prayers give you a framework for your prayers. We have added Scripture verses from the Bible so you can commit to memory a short text as your shout of affirmation or praise. As you develop your faith these words can become stepping stones in your relationship with God.

Lord, you are wonderful

Lord, as I wake for a new day,
I want you to know you're right up there,
    topping the list of those
        I honour and admire.
You are awesome.

I look at the wonder of your creation,
    its colour, design and purpose,
        and its constant renewal.

I remember all the love
    you show to each and every one of us
        in the life and death and resurrection
        of Jesus Christ.

I stop and feel
    the presence of your Holy Spirit,
        filling my heart with joy and peace.

Then I know for sure, my God,
    that you are truly wonderful.

A Scripture verse: *Praise the Lord, O my soul:*
    O Lord my God you are great indeed.   *(Ps 104:1)*

Beginning the day

I'm in a rush, God,
> but please stick by me today
>> to guide me,
>> to help me.

Support me all the day
> with your everlasting love.

Thanks God, for when you're beside me
> I know all will be well.

A Scripture verse: *I will sing of your power O Lord,*
each morning acclaim your love.   *(Ps 59:17)*

At the end of day

God, you rested after you had created the world.
I've had a busy day
       and now I am exhausted,
           – yet there is still so much to do.
I ask you to calm me down
       and give me the energy
           to do those tasks that are most urgent.

....

Thanks God, for this day,
       for health and strength,
       for family and friends,
       for growth and learning.
May I rest tonight in your love
       and wake to serve you tomorrow.

A Scripture verse: *I will lie down and sleep in peace;*
          for you alone, O Lord, make me dwell in safety. (Ps 4:8)

I'm in a crisis, Lord
　　and it's like this

．．．．．．．．．．．．．．．．．．．．．．．．．．．．．．．．．．．．．．．

Now I've told you,
　　I'm beginning to feel better.

Dear God, be near me,
　　to calm me,
　　to clear my mind,
　　to take away my fear
　　and to show me the options
　　　　to move forward.

Give me your strength and wisdom, God,
　　for you are my friend and my guide.

Crisis, Lord

A Scripture verse:　　*Trust in God at all times,*
pour out your heart before God;
for God is a refuge for us.　　*(Ps 62:8)*

Lord, I'm really sorry

Lord Jesus, I'm really sorry.
    This is what happened … …

I'm sorry for the wrong I have done.
    I ask to be forgiven.
I will learn from this
    and with your help
        try to choose the better option next time.
Give me your Spirit
    and assure me of your love.

Thank you, Lord,
    for your forgiveness.

A Scripture verse: *I will confess my sin.*
                      I am sorry for my wrong doings.   *(Ps 38:18)*

Jesus, keep me loving

Jesus, I lost it today
    and now I am both furious and embarrassed.
    Let me tell you … …

What would you have said, Jesus?
How would you have handled it?
I suppose love would have been your guide
    but that was not how it was with me.

Lord Jesus, teach me how to love,
    to say to others words I could hear from them,
    to judge others in the way you would judge me,
        with understanding and with love.

A Scripture verse: *Let love for one another continue.*   *(Hebrews 13:1)*

THANKS

Hey God,

It's been a great day.
I'm thrilled.
I want to tell you about it.

It was cool when ... ...
Things went really well because ... ...
I had a great time at ... ...

Wow! I'm so happy –
do you share my joy?

Thank you, my God,
for all the many gifts you have given me,
for laughter and good times,
for family and friends to share my success,
and for the growing confidence I've found in myself.

Thank you, God,
for your love to me.
I don't deserve it!
But then I don't need to.
It's your gift so freely given.
Thank you, God, for loving me.

A Scripture verse: *Let the peace of Christ rule in your hearts, and be thankful. (Colossians 3:15)*

Txt Gd

GR8 & PWRFL GD U HAV GIDED ME
N DA RITE DRCTN EVR SNC I WAZ BRN

PLS CNTNU TRIEN 2 GIDE ME N DA RITE WY

JC I ASK U 2 HR DIS PRYR

AMN

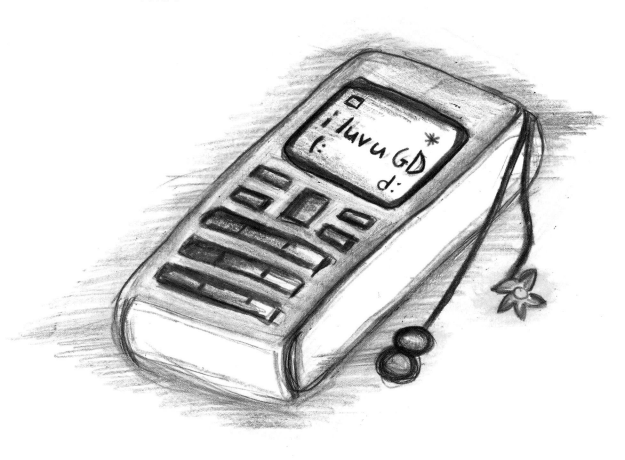

A Scripture verse: *God will be our guide forever.*   (Ps 48:14)

The Lord's Prayer

Our Father who art in heaven,
    hallowed be thy name,
    thy kingdom come,
    thy will be done,
on earth as it is in heaven.
Give us this day our daily bread
And forgive us our trespasses
    as we forgive those who trespass
        against us.
And lead us not into temptation
    but deliver us from evil.
Amen.

If you know another form of this prayer, paste it in here.

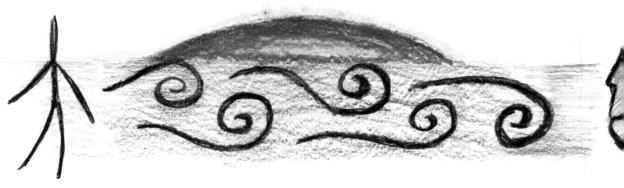

In Conversation with God

There are many issues that every young person faces as they grow up. God so understands and loves us that we can speak with God about such issues in our times of reflective prayer. As Jesus shared our human life so we will want to talk with him about how life is for us.

We asked a group of young people in our church to draw up a short list of the topics they felt were most important to cover in these prayers. With the help of Olivia and Lloyd, we developed the text so that you could explore the issues in God's presence. The words provide a starting point for such conversations and, in time, you will find your own words as you share the issues you face with God.

When you have spoken your prayers leave a time of silence so that you can listen to God's voice telling you how much you are loved and valued, and prompting you to live your life according to God's will, made known to us in Jesus Christ.

Having fun

Jesus, they tell me some of your stories made everyone laugh.
It must have been fun to be among your friends.

Thank you for the fun times in life,
        the occasions of success and high fives
        when we share laughter and jokes
        and celebrate the good times together,
        especially I remember when … …

But Jesus,
        they tell me some people laughed at you on the Cross
                and made jokes about you being a king.
        Help me never to have fun
        at the expense of those who look weak or helpless.
        Help me to cool my tongue
                when it is tempted to poke fun at others.

So, Jesus, give me your Spirit of joy
        to celebrate the good things of life,
and give me your Spirit of self-control
        to avoid laughing at others.

In that Spirit you and I can celebrate together.

Lord, I looked
in the mirror

Lord, I looked in the mirror today
and saw myself.
I'm not certain any more how I want to look.

Everyone seems to be trying out new trends in clothes
        and new hair styles.
They want to change their shape
        and strut their stuff
        – to look like pop stars.
But does it matter whether I follow this or that fashion?

Where is the real me in all this,
        the me that you know and respect,
        the me whose qualities don't depend on
        fashion?

Lord, give me the self-assurance to dress
well,
        to eat well,
        to show I care about myself.
Help me also to display my inner qualities,
        shaped by your Holy Spirit.

That's the me I want to see in the mirror
today.

Being a friend

Jesus, I'm glad you came to earth to share our human life.
I'm glad because you'll understand about friendship.
You know how some friends are hard to understand.
I do like my friends … … and … …,
but so often I feel I'm the one in the middle.
I hear the secrets, the plans of one or the other,
but when I'm told 'Don't say anything'
I feel disloyal to my other friend.
Do you understand, Jesus, or is it just me?

Give me your love and guidance
to feel strong in myself,
to make wise choices
and to say the right things.

Give me your Spirit to value these friends
and to develop new friendships.
Above all, Jesus, thank you for being a supportive friend to me,
wise, loyal and true.

Lord, I want to understand

Lord, it's exciting learning new things.
Your world is a wonderful place
      where the curious go star trekking
          to trace its patterns and its surprises.

Thank you for insight to see
      and a brain to learn
      and a mind to make sense of
      so much knowledge.

I ask you, Lord,
      to help me understand
      your purpose in creating me
      and the world in which I live;
and help me to use my knowledge
      to make your world a better place.

So may I honour you with a mind
      dedicated to your service.

It all went wrong

Lord,
I stuffed up today!
　　　　It all went wrong.
Where were you when … …?

Now, I feel screwed up
　　and alone.

　　I guess you were there beside me
　　　　but I forgot your support,
　　　　your concern for me.

Please help me, Lord.
　　I made a mistake
　　　　but I have got to pick myself up again.

　　　　　Knowing how much you care for me,
　　　　　　with your help and guidance,
　　　　I can say I'm sorry,
　　　　　　receive forgiveness,
　　　　　　　be renewed by your Spirit
　　　　　and make a new start.

One world, many cultures

God, you made us all to live in one world,
    although we come from many different backgrounds and cultures.
Thank you for the diversity within the one human race.

I have a brilliant group of friends;
    many were born here
    but some have come from other countries.
Thank you for these special friends.

Sometimes we notice great differences in our ways of doing things,
    in our family customs,
    in the ways we express our faith,
but underneath these differences my friends are pretty much like me.
We share the same hopes, the same fears, the same dreams.

Help me always to respect those who come from different cultures
    and to offer friendship and understanding,
        so that we overcome racism
        and work together in harmony,
        for the good of all your world.
In Jesus' name I pray.

Reaching out

Creator God,
    I can imagine your hand reaching out
    to make contact with each one of us
      in the world you have created.
Out of love you want us to know you
    and to respond with love and affection.

Family and friends hold hands
    and I equally value their touch
      when life is full of joy,
      when life is full of challenges.

Caring God,
      may I have the faith and courage
      to grasp your hand.
When I am in danger of falling,
      hold me.
When I want to rush off madly,
      hold me back.
When I am too timid to seek the path to life,
      lead me in the right direction.

Lord God, I put my hand in yours.

Christ! They said your name

Lord Jesus Christ, I heard your name on
the TV last night
        and it wasn't said with reverence.

I didn't like it.

It hurt.

At your Crucifixion men scorned you
        and spat on you,
but the soldier watching the way you died
        knew that you were the Son of God.

Help me only to use your name
        with reverence, in worship and in prayer,
                to show how much I love and honour you.

Guide me as I witness among my family and friends
        so that all in our society may come to know you
                as our Saviour, Jesus Christ.

Call now – there's a cheap deal!
Buy now – and pay later!
Eat this! Drink that! Wear those!

TV ads

Ads, ads and more ads,
    and each one shouted at me.
Does everyone want to help me
    or are they just after my money?
How true are these ads?
Stop the shouting – I want to think!

Jesus, you didn't have to suffer TV ads.
You said that if I follow you and become
    your true disciple,
then the truth will set me free.

I want to be free:
    free of advertising pressures,
    free of tempting offers and unreal change,
    free to serve you and your kingdom.
Jesus, give me this freedom through your spirit of truth.

Dear God,
everyone says that growing up can cause a few problems.
Tell me about it!

Growing up

Now I'm ... ... years old
    I am beginning to find that I want to make
        some of my own decisions
    and not just let others say
        where I should be,
        whether I can come,
        what I ought to do.

My family have helped me so much in the past.
May I always remember and understand
        their longing for all to be well in my world,
        but how can I help them see
        I am changing and want to take charge of my life?

So, God, I ask for your guidance.
    Help me to talk to ... ...
    They are wise and will listen
        as I tell them how I feel.
    Guide us to work out a plan
        and set some boundaries
        that will help me and my family.

May I listen to the words of your Son, Jesus,
so that my choices follow his path of life.

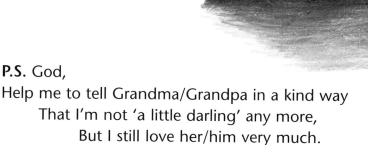

P.S. God,
Help me to tell Grandma/Grandpa in a kind way
    That I'm not 'a little darling' any more,
        But I still love her/him very much.

Jesus,
      there were times in your life
            when you wanted to be alone.
I've read of others who felt like this too.

We have a happy family
      and there are lots of people about,
            many relatives and good friends.
I like joining in with them all.

I want to be alone

But there are times when
    I want to be alone,
    to have some space –
        time to think,
        time to be,
        time to do my thing.

In those times
    let your Holy Spirit
    guide and inspire me,
    fill me with love
    and give me inner peace.

        Then being alone will send me back to the crowd
        ready to share all I have discovered.

My body's changing

God my creator,
    I look in the mirror
        and see my body's changing.
I'm growing up – that's brilliant!

But it isn't all great.
    There are times –
        when I seem to get out of step with my family;
        when I say things I don't mean to say;
        when I do things I don't want to do;
        when I slam my bedroom door shut –
            it's a wonder it still opens!

I'm often on edge – sometimes I want to be alone,
    other times I want to be in with the crowd.
My emotions are all over the place.

Creator God, you made me,
    so you will understand what I'm saying.
Help me to remember that you made me to be creative
    and, as my body is changing, so I can also grow
        in maturity,
        in understanding,
        in my emotions
        and in my unique personality.

May I accept the wonder of these changes
    as part of your divine plan for me,
and in these times of rapid growth and constant change
    feel the security of your unchanging love
        and the support of my family and friends.

Creator God, give me your Spirit so that I can grow stable and strong,
    and serve you well in the years to come.

Dam' it!

Lord, it didn't work out.
I had raised my hopes so high
    and now they are dashed.
I set my goals to succeed
    and I missed out.
It wasn't anyone's fault,
    it just turned out that way;
but the result was devastating just the same.
    Dam' it.

Jesus, you know how it feels.
You had high hopes
    that people would change their ways,
    and live according to God's plan,
        and they killed you on a Cross.
You had high hopes for your disciples;
    when you needed them most,
        they fled in fear.
How can I learn from you
    the way to deal with disappointment?

You had one word for it – **Resurrection**:
    putting life back into the situation,
    making a whole new beginning
        in God's almighty power.

Jesus, give me this 'resurrection',
    new energy for life,
    new ways for living,
    new hopes of success,
    new faith in you.

Jesus, breathe new life into me.

Saying 'no'

The red traffic light tells me to stop.
    It is stupid to ignore it and go forward.
    You'll get hurt. That's obvious.

It is so easy to race through life ignoring the warnings:
    one drug is called 'speed'
        and only leads to a crash;
    peer pressure can take you down wrong roads;
    some relationships only leave you dented;
    drinking and driving is dangerous;
    alcohol can mess up your decisions at other times.

Jesus, help me to know when to say 'no'
    to those things that will only cause
        damage in my life.

The trouble is, Lord, that saying 'no'
appears
    to lead to such a dull life,
    to make you miss out on the kicks,
    to let others think of you as childish,
    and to leave you out of the group.

But, Jesus, I don't want to make mistakes
    just to prove I'm cool;
        that's stupid!

So help me value myself enough
    to have the courage to say 'no'
    and to follow your way
        – that makes good sense to me.

Our friendship is broken

Jesus, I wonder how you felt on that night
    when Judas Iscariot left the table
        and went out to betray you.

Did you want to run after him and say,
    'Come back, we'll start again?'
Did you feel isolated and a failure?
Jesus, I want to ask you so many questions,
    for this is how I feel today.

Jesus, I feel devastated now I have broken up with ... ...
    I feel all alone and hurt.
        I guess I might have hurt ... ... too.
I know the bond of our friendship is broken
    and there is no turning back.

Jesus, walk beside me,
    give me renewed confidence in myself,
    and help me to make new friends.
Maybe I should choose more carefully,
    so guide me in my choices.
Teach me to care for my friendships,
    neither asking too much nor giving too much,
    able to share the ups and downs,
    walking together along life's paths,
        as you did Jesus, with your friends.

I'm sick ...

Christ the healer, they brought the sick to you
    for healing and new life.
I need your help now,
    I'm sick and I'm scared.

The doctor says I'm ill.
    I could have told Doc that.
It's obvious.
It's a pain. I feel wiped out,
    drained of energy.
It's awful lying here in bed.
I'm missing out on so many things.
And I don't know how long it will be
    before I am better.

... and I'm scared

Loving God, I need you.
Give me your peace,
    the assurance that you care for me.
Work with the body
    you have created
        and bring it back to health.
Take away my fear,
    renew my trust in you
        and in my future.

Bless all who care for me.

Let your Spirit flow through my body
    and make it whole again.

Jesus, my tears flow.
  I'm so sad because ... ...

Jesus, the Gospel record tells us
  you too were often sad –
      when people rejected or hurt you,
      when one of your best friends died.
  The Gospels also tell us that your presence
      comforted your friends in their times of grief.

My tears flow

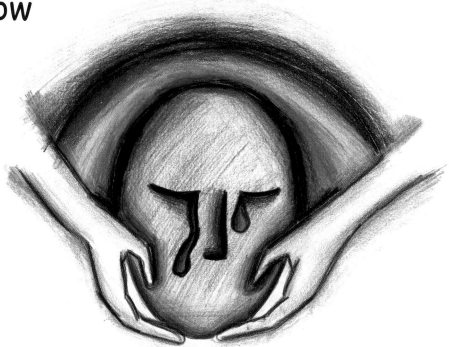

Jesus, be near me now
  and with your strong arm around me
      support me while my tears flow.

I'm sad because I love ... ...
      Enfold them in your love
          and give them the joy of your eternal presence;
  For Jesus you are my God
      and I trust you,
          now and for ever.

My Prayers for Others

Notes on Intercessions

Jesus invites us to share in his work of upholding the world and its people in prayer so that God's purpose may be fulfilled. We invite you to share in this work of intercession – that is praying for others – by regularly using these prayers and inserting in them the actual situations known to you. Prayers are about real people and real situations so include them in your prayers.

Prayers of intercession are effective because we are joining our prayers to those of Jesus Christ, whose Spirit and power are at work in God's world. After you have prayed with Jesus for family and friends make sure you tell those you have named in prayer that you have interceded for them. This will bring them strength, comfort and God's peace.

My family

Jesus, in your life on earth you knew
    the love and the strength,
    the life and the security
        of being part of a family.

        I pray for my family … …
           and for all families.

        I pray that your love may be shared,
         love that shows both
            tenderness and strength,
            discipline and freedom,
            respect and understanding.

Help our family to learn
    to give as well as receive,
    to share the tasks that have to be done,
    to contribute honesty and fun,
    participation and delight
        in the special times we share as a family.

Dear God, thank you for my family
    and bless us all.

My school

Jesus, you were a Rabbi, a teacher.
Thank you for my school,
       where there are so many opportunities
          for learning.

Help my school to be a place
       where we can learn the truth –
          the truth about our world
          and the truth about ourselves.

Give skill and wisdom to our teachers
    and give us all your spirit of kindness
       to support one another.

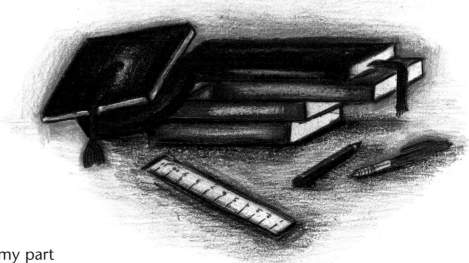

Help me to play my part
       to make my school a happy place
    where we learn to succeed
       without putting others down,
    where we learn to face disappointment
       without giving up,
    where we learn the facts
       without dismissing imagination.

Lord, you call us to be your disciples,
       bless us in our learning at school.

God's church

God, I love to visit our church.
It is made holy with the prayers
        of so many people.
They find you there
through your Word and Sacraments.

Bless my church. Keep it holy.
May young and old honour you
        in worship and in service.

Help the congregation recognise
        that we, young people,
        have a full place in your church.

Guide our leaders … …
        who share their faith with us
        and teach us your Holy Word.

Give us your Spirit to put into practice
        what we learn
and give us your courage to witness
        to your place in our lives.
Then we will be your true disciples,
        followers of Jesus Christ our Lord.

God's world

When I watch the news on TV,
the world you made, God,
seems to be in crisis.

With your Son, Jesus Christ, I pray
for the world you still love.
Restrain its violence and its plunder;
point out to nations
the stupidity of fighting and greed;
guide our leaders
in the ways of peace and conservation.

Support the needy,
feed the hungry,
comfort the crying
and uphold those working
to build community
and to care for creation.

And as I pray like this,
I know I must be part
of the answer to our prayers.

Help me to be a partner with you in your world
and to act with your wisdom and love,
so that the world follows your plan –
where all creatures have their place
and all people live in harmony
and your kingdom comes on earth,
as your will is done in heaven.

Those who are sad

Risen Christ,
    my friend / family member is sad because … …

Give them your comfort and support,
    your gifts of compassion and hope.

Help me to show sympathy
    even though I don't quite understand
        the depth of their feelings in grief.
Inspire me to say the right words
    and to do small acts of kindness
        to show them that I share their sorrow.

Good Shepherd, speak your words of peace to those who are sad
    and renew their trust in your guiding hand
        in the valley of sorrow.

Those who are sick

Jesus, you healed the sick,
    when their friends brought them into your presence.
Hear my prayer as I pray for … …
    and all who are sick.
Give them your healing power and your loving presence.

Bring to them caring doctors and nurses
    to help them with the skills of medicine.

May your peace give them strength and patience
    to allow their bodies to heal.
May your love make them whole again
    so that they can give thanks to you for health and healing.

So Christ my Lord, bless the sick today.